MY BODY IS A JUNKYARD

Aitch Alexandar

GLASSSPIDERPUBLISHING

ISBN: 979-8-9851773-3-6
Library of Congress Control Number:
2021925237

Edited by Vince Font
Cover design by Jane Font
Published by Glass Spider Publishing
www.glassspiderpublishing.com

To my father, Jack:
I am funny & weird just like you.

To my mother, Carol Jean:
These words & expressed emotions are for you.

To my older sister, Nicki:
I am happy & loved thanks to you.

To teachers everywhere:
Never doubt the impact you have on a young
person.

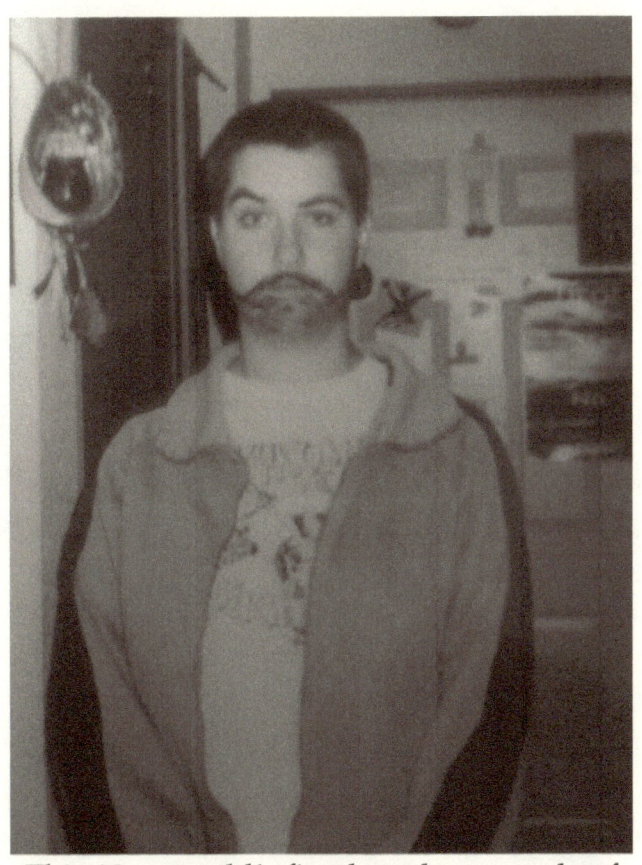

This 18-year-old's first beard was made of
the finest marker.

Author's Note

These pages of poems come with a degree
of caution. Since we're all a mixed bag of
emotions & experiences, I want you, dear
reader, to know up front before you
journey into my world that some of the
topics include imagery about:

  Death, loss, addiction, abuse, neglect,
  trauma, suicide, prison, murder,
  violence, divorce, body & gender
  dysphoria, transphobia, anxiety,
  profanity, blasphemy, and sex.

This collection also includes images of
healing, hope, love, rebirth, humor,
transformation, and of course, cats.

–Aitch Alexandar

Contents

i: FRAME

TW: DYSPHORIA, TRANSPHOBIA, PRISON, DEATH, LOSS, ABUSE

For all the gender warriors; all the loved ones lost; all the complicated families; and Dr. Doreen.

UNTIL ONE DAY

when I was a girl-boy,
I would run around
with all the other boys
and pray to god
that he had made
a mistake;
until one day,
I learned that
god smites those
who cast doubt upon
his magnificence.

when I was a boy-girl,
I would wrap up my body
in disgust and hide;
until one day,
I fed it to the wolves
inside my own head.

when I was a girl,
I would lock up my soul
in a dungeon and cry;
until one day,
I became death and killed
everything I touched.

when I was a boy,
I finally grew up
tall and brave;
until one day,
I was born into a man
with love and kindness
for myself.

FUNERAL FOR A DEADNAME

Deadname (verb)
1. To call someone, specifically a transgender or
non-binary person, by the name they were given
at birth after they no longer go by that name.
2. To commit an act of emotional violence,
intentionally or unintentionally, against a
transgender or non-binary person by calling
them by their former name.

Rest In Peace:

To the name that I never wanted.
To the name that never fit me.
To the name that I never liked.

To the name that my mom gave me.
To the name that my dad
can never say again.
To the name that my beloved
used to call me.

To the name that nobody new in my life
needs to learn.
To the name that should never
ever be queried.
To the name that doesn't even exist
for me anymore.

CONCRETE MAMA (THE WALLS)

in my hometown,
there is a place
called concrete mama
whose concrete walls
surround all the
concrete hearts;
inside the walls,
are all the people
who guard the roads
never taken
by all the lives
hopelessly
forsaken.

DIGNITY

death is
a precious reminder that
kindness
always matters.

ROCK

I never knew you well
or saw you be funny
until I watched you die
in the hospital bed.

I still miss you.

I never knew what it was like
to have a mom
because you knew drugs
better than you ever knew me.

I still love you.

I remember your anger
and how you always
told me, *stop crying*
or I will give you
something
to cry about!

I'm still afraid of angry people.

I remember how you
would push me off the couch
when I was little
and in need of comfort or love.

I still push others away.

I remember all the good times too
but they're not the ones
that gave me my strength.

I'm still a rock just like you.

MY CHEST IS A CASTLE

my chest is a castle
with strong walls that
keep my soft heart safe
from people who might do it harm
like lovers
or worse
family.

ii: PICK-N-PULL

TW: LOSS, DEATH, PROFANITY, SEX

*For Chris & Ethan; nurses, especially Jen
Robertson—a real badass; and Ilanit.*

MY BODY IS A JUNKYARD

my body is a junkyard
with broken bits
scattered all around
and mixed in
with all the moving parts—
the used parts & the abused parts
the happy parts & the sad parts
the scared parts & the brave parts
the lost parts & the found parts
the past parts & the future parts
the cracked parts & the sane parts
not every part is pretty or perfect
but they're all discounted
and they all work
mostly
everything is marked as-is
and of course
no returns

FIRST LOVE: I

sometimes I still
hear your silly laugh
and glimpse your sweet smile
and smell your favorite scent
sometimes my eyes
see you flicker
in a flame of someone else
like a candle vigil
your essence remains
a love still remembered

REBIRTH

one by one
my life fell down
like a shitty game of dominoes
my marriage died
my mother died
my cat died
my
cat
fucking
died.

but out of this wreckage
and out of this pain
i built a whole new me
and i am stronger now
and i am braver now
and i am here now
i
am
fucking
here.

WALMART BUST

I took you both to see mom
as she lay dying in the hospital
afterwards we left to get some food
mostly to feed my own survivor's guilt
one of you went in the front
the other through the back
one of you dodged
the camera
the other triggered
an unknown alert
I remember thinking
how sad our hearts were
but at least we were together
I remember temporarily forgetting who
you both really were
besides my older brothers

and just like in the movies
I was brought back to reality
with flashing cars out of nowhere
and cops and warrants
and finally one of you in cuffs
and just like a sad country song
I was left with broken promises
to pick up
all the broken pieces
inside my
broken heart.

GIVEN

a glass of water—
given, as a comfort
behind a closed door.
take as much time
as you need—
given, as a kind gesture
for the pain ahead.
holding someone as they
take their last breath—
given, as a gift
to a dying loved one.
a kiss on the forehead—
given, as a last goodbye.

JUST WONDERING

when I think about sex
I like to think of it as
taking a walk
sometimes you take a really long walk
other times just a short one
maybe you take a casual walk once a month
or multiple walks a week
then of course there's
the occasional spicy walk
with toys or sultry secrets shared
and don't forget about
the birthday or anniversary walks
as long as you want
or need
or crave
to take a walk
any kind of walk
then you're completely normal
and absolutely natural
and perfectly healthy
according to the world

and Jesus
or whatever religion
you do or do not believe in
but what if you often forget to take a walk
or you only take one
when it's someone else's idea
or you used to take a lot of walks
but now you're sort of retired
or worse yet
what if you take walks because you have to
under pressure
or duress
or disappointment
maybe the thought of walking
never really even
organically
crosses your mind very much
but no matter the reason
if you don't walk
regularly
or even irregularly
then are you even
normal

or natural

or healthy

or worse yet

lovable

are there other non-walkers

just like you

roaming around

out there

in the wild world

walking

just because

they must

and wondering to themselves

just wondering

if they're the only one.

iii: ENGINE

TW: DYSPHORIA, ANXIETY, DEATH, TRAUMA, VIOLENCE

For Maeve; Shari; Steve J.; Little Bit; and Kellie.

CONFLICTED

sometimes

my heart is

like a dog—

forgiving and hopeful.

other times

my heart is

like a cat—

ferocious and homicidal.

TOUCH

if you touch me gently
with your eyes
then I can swim
in rainbow rays of bliss.
if you touch me softly
with your lips
then I can breathe
a new life into your soul.
if you touch me passionately
with your body
then I can give
you back unto yourself.
if you touch me fully
with your love
then I can taste
your essence.
if you touch me deeply
with your pain
then I can feel
inside you.

but if you touch me
even slightly
with your judgment
then I cannot
do anything
at all.

SOMETIMES (ANXIETY)

I hate it when
you tell me,
you'll never be good enough
or when you say,
your body is ugly and weak.
I hate the sound of your voice
and the curves of your hips.
I hate down below
and how you still bleed.
sometimes I hate everything about you;
but then I remember *you* aren't even me
even if sometimes our voices blend into
one.

just relax, you yell.
don't be so uptight, you rage.
your anxiety gives me anxiety, you scream.
you are just remnants from other people,
slinking around like shadows in my mind,
infecting who I think I am
and how I feel
or how I think I feel
or how I feel I think.

CODEPENDENCY

To my buried mother:

I don't owe you an apology
for speaking up
and saying, please protect me.

To my buried brother:

I don't regret
fighting for a good life
and wishing, please forget me.

To my buried trauma:

I don't miss your toxic ways
and the constant begging,
please love me.

Please love me.
Please love me.
Please love me.

WORRIES WILD: I

Your dad is crazy. "He made a list of
people to kill," my cousin taunts. "And
Grandma keeps a small Beretta in her purse
just in case she's on that list." *Really? She's
not afraid of anything*, I think. Imagining her
Baptist body literally filled with fire &
brimstone. Picturing her chasing my
brother around the house with a wooden
spoon. Remembering how she washed my
mouth out with soap when I didn't come
running to the table for dinner. "Hold on,
Grandma, I'm coloring," I had foolishly
replied. Her footsteps then roaring wildly
through the house as she ran to get me. To
teach me manners. I was ten years old. *She's
afraid of my dad?* "We all knew he was off,"
everyone else shares after the fact. "He was
such a sweet boy," my Jehovah's Witness
grandma confides. "Always loved
baseball."

FIRST LOVE: II

And even after
all these years
I think missing you
still gives me purpose;
and loving others
still gives me hope.

FORGIVENESS

I forgive the pain that swallowed you up
and birthed a copy of you
for us to call Mom.

I forgive the hate that you must have felt
at a world that cut you so deep
you bled until your children bled too.

MOMMY ISSUES

When you yell at me my whole body jerks.
                    I freeze.
                        I can't breathe.

I want to run and hide
and lock the bathroom door behind me.
                    I can't tell the difference
                    between a new pain
                    and an old one.

You can yell
but
please
don't yell
at me.

FIRST LOVE: III

As
life
soldiers on
the
head
also
moves on.

But
the
heart
always
remains
fond.

iv: TIRES

TW: LOSS, PROFANITY, SUICIDE, DEATH, PRISON, BLASPHEMY, VIOLENCE

For Billy & Tracii.

DEATH OF A UNION

after you died, marriage,
i wallowed in my own misery;
i made shitty choices,
and i drank and i fucked,
and i drank and i fucked.

i tried to forget you
by trying to kill me,
slowly and with indifference.
i wanted to die, to really die.
because all i knew,
all i could remember,
after seven long years
was us.

who was i even before i was us?

but eventually i started living again.
and i started remembering
who i was and who i could be
and i am
happy now.

MAGICALLY

The last thing I said to you was, you don't
have to fight anymore.
I held you in my arms for two hours.
You died over and over.
The nurses told me that this would happen.
And my mind understood that the body
starts and stops.
The body starts and stops.
But my heart didn't understand.
My heart. It didn't understand.
It felt like you died in my arms and then
magically came back to life.

But then you died again.

But then you magically came back to life.

But then you died again.

But then you magically came back to life.

But then you died again.

And finally you died.

You died. Finally. Died.

No magic left.

No magic.

Left.

A FUNERAL & A KIDNEY: I

Socks shuffling to the Nurses' Station.
A voice whispering, *I think my mom just
died.*
Feet slowly walking out of the hospital,
trancelike.
A phone suddenly ringing and a voice
calling from prison.
Screams of anger upon hearing the patient
died minutes ago.
The voice on the phone yelling, *why couldn't
she wait for me!*
Drinking beer alone in the hotel room later
that night.
Placing the heart in a figurative tourniquet.
Trying hard to prepare for surviving the
weeks ahead.
Calling all the loved ones.
Remembering to keep breathing.

420 LINCOLN STREET

If there really is a god (or goddess or a collective of gods) then the Alleged Almighty has a twisted sense of humor and an ironic obsession with foreshadowing.

Like Dad showing up to grandma's house smelling of pot while unwittingly wearing a D.A.R.E. t-shirt he bought at a second-hand store.

Like finding the deed to the house that Mom and Dad owned before he went to prison—420 Lincoln Street.

Like learning that Dad only had the gun he used that night because some guy couldn't pay for his pot. It was just collateral.

Like hearing that a few months before that fatal incident the cops raided 420 Lincoln Street to seize all the pot. But they didn't seize the gun.

WORRIES WILD: II

When I was 13, I met my dad after he got
out of prison. He bought me a puffy Miami
Dolphins jacket and we watched The Lion
King in the theater together. He cried
silently when he talked. Tears steaming like
I do when I'm upset but fighting the urge to
cry. Soft-spoken & tender-hearted just like
me. Dark brown hair & big blue eyes also
just like me. He didn't look like a murderer.
Will I grow up to kill someone too? When I
was 14, he came to my drill meet. Gave me
a baseball mitt that he had greased and
wrapped a rubber band around. Wanted to
play catch so we did but I didn't like it. I
didn't care for sports then. I still don't like
them. But I love my dad. He's nothing like
they all said he was except he really does
love baseball.

A FUNERAL & A KIDNEY: II

I paid my Baptist grandpa to have my mom
placed in the family plot;
later at the funeral home, he asked me if I
was still gay,
or if I was finally ready to come back to
Jesus.
He reminded me I used to be such a great
child of God.
I'm sorry, grandpa, I whispered back to him
with my head cast downward.
But in that moment I wanted to loudly
declare to him and the universe,
*I'm fine the way I am! And fuck your fucking
God anyways!*
I didn't of course because no matter what I
loved my grandpa
even if his love for me was tied to my
everlasting soul.

Do you think your mom took the Lord into her
heart before she died?
He asked me softly, clearly distraught.
Maybe, grandpa. The hospital chaplain spoke to
her in her room alone.
He brightened up when he heard this—
the promise of eternal salvation seeming to
comfort his grief.

v: SCRAPS

TW: LOSS, DEATH, ADDICTION

For Micah; AJL; Tyson; and JDH.

TOXIC WITH A SIDE OF SALT

some people burn tires to stay warm
others do it to stay angry
either way the world dies a little
and your lungs cry a little too
like they do living in Salt Lake City.

my dad says tires can burn forever
I know that's hyperbole
but both earth and body remember
because toxic with a side of salt
is still toxic.

UNCONDITIONAL LOVE

in sickness and in health
or when it's no longer fun anymore.
I know that my wounds
wounded you too and made your heart
slowly break into little bits
of sadness,
desperately,
trying to love me
into wholeness.

thank you for leaving
so that I could
finally heal myself.

THE BUTTHOLE DOCTORS

I walked into my mom's hospital room
to a level of laughter that distracted us
from all the pain
she felt in her declining body
like I felt in my decaying heart.
the butthole doctors washed her butt
and it felt good, she sang all night.

I walked into my mom's hospital room
to a level of screams that pierced
right through
her wilting body
like it did my withering heart.
"No more morphine for her,"
an asshole doctor said,
"She's just a junkie waiting for a fix,"
his judging glance roared.

I walked into my mom's hospital room
to a level of frost that chilled
her beaten-down body
like it did my broken heart.
"When was her last bowel movement?"
another asshole demanded,
coldly ignoring my mom's cries,
"Doctor, doctor, what's wrong with me?"

A FUNERAL & A KIDNEY: III

momma,
brother is sick too
he says he needs
a new kidney, please
to use and abuse
with meth until death.

momma,
you're not even buried yet
but brother needs
a new kidney, please
to use and abuse
with meth until death.

momma,
brother wants me
to give him
a new kidney, please
to use and abuse
with meth until death.

momma,
please forgive me
but I can't give brother
a new kidney, please
to use and abuse
with meth until death.

A VAGINA WALKS INTO THE MEN'S ROOM

a vagina cloaked in a beard
and jeans
and a ball cap
and really cool glasses
wrapped in a cape
full of fear and trepidation
walks into the men's room
to pee
just to fucking pee
but there's politics
in peeing now.
the vagina opens the stall
and jumps in the air, squealing
there's a penis in the stall
already peeing

the vagina yelps,
oh, shit, I'm sorry
and runs outside
to tell all the other vaginas
and all the other penises.
one penis confesses,
that's called urinal overflow
the vagina laughs
and then cries
then pees themself
because there's politics
in peeing now.

A KITTY WALKS INTO THE MEN'S ROOM

a kitty cloaked in a beard
and jeans
and a ball cap
and really cool glasses
wrapped in a cape
full of fear and trepidation
walks into the men's room
to wee
just to freakin' wee
but there's politics
in weeing now.
the kitty opens the stall
and jumps in the air, squealing
there's a doodle in the stall
already weeing

the kitty yelps,
oh, heck, I'm sorry
and runs outside
to tell all the other kitties
and all the other doodles.
one doodle confesses,
that's called urinal overflow
the kitty laughs
and then cries
then wees themself
because there's politics
in weeing now.

TOMBSTONE

you know that feeling you get when you
start falling in love?
hormones flying
fantasies whirling
the moon & the sun
all perfect in their rotations
every single song you hear
lights up your soul
you want to recite poetry
you want to write poetry
you dress up
and maybe even add a dollop of scent
you see rainbows everywhere you go
and four-leaf clovers too
you are one
obnoxious lovesick cliche after another
you know what I mean?

that's exactly
how I feel
about cats & pizza
every single cat I meet is a rainbow
even the evil ones
especially the evil ones
every single pizza I see is a poem
even the shitty ones
when I die my tombstone will read:
he probably loved cats & pizza too much
but he sure was happy.

Acknowledgments

Thank you to all my friends & family for always believing in me even when I was hemorrhaging emotionally and fucking up my life. I finally got the help that I needed because of you all.

Thank you to every teacher I ever had for making my life brighter. School gave me the stability & enrichment that I didn't get at home. You are the why & the how I overcame the odds stacked against me.

Thank you to Aunt Connie, Deanna & Dave for always loving me as I am.

Thank you to Nat, Shannon, Asmita, Moho, Taylor & Maggie, and Ilanit for catching me when I fell.

Thank you to Nicki for taking in a displaced 14-year-old kid and changing the direction of their entire life for the better. I love you.

Thank you to Shari & Ken for the decades of hearty laughs & mild mischief.

Thank you to PC & Ali for challenging me & opening my heart to languages. Besos.

Thank you to Shira and her whole community of family & friends for helping me raise my teenaged niece. It really did take a village or two.

Thank you to Billy & Tracii for all the fun & friendship.

Thank you to Wasatch Commons Cohousing for being the instant extended family a new parental unit needed after moving to Utah with a teenager in tow.

Thank you to Full Circle Yoga & Therapy for helping me heal my body & mind.

Thank you to Amy, Giuliana, Moudi, Taylor, and Nan for creating safe & wonderful spaces throughout the SLC community for all of us to bravely share pieces of ourselves.

Thank you to The Bee & KRCL for letting me share my story about my mother. Part of that story is included in my poem now titled "Rebirth." You can listen to the entire story told live on stage by going to the RadioActive episode on KRCL, which aired August 29, 2018. The Bee section of this episode begins at around the 23-minute mark.

Thank you to Dr. D., Kade, and K. Scott Forman for mentoring me with a mix of kindness & snark.

Thank you to Vince Font & Glass Spider Publishing for making my book dreams come true.

Thank you to my cadre of cats who fill my house with hairballs & litter crumbs, and my heart with unbridled joy & laughter.

About the Author

Aitch Alexandar is an openly queer, transmasculine human originally from Walla Walla, Washington. (Yes, that's a real place.) He is a Navy veteran with 20 years of experience as a professional polyglot who currently resides in the Salt Lake City metro area. Although he now identifies as male, he likes to think that if his vagina were a person, they would identify as non-binary. His poems depict his experiences of being socialized as female as a child, coming out as trans much later in life, as well as the non-judgmental emotions of someone who has spent a lifetime loving family members addicted to drugs. He's awkward, funny, and probably too obsessed with pizza & cats. Also, this is not his cat.

Instagram: @aitch_writes_stuff

About the Publisher

Glass Spider Publishing was founded in 2016 by writer Vince Font to help independent and self-published authors reach readers through professionally edited and artfully designed books. The company is headquartered in Ogden, Utah, but has published authors throughout the world including the United States, Canada, England, and Kenya.

www.glassspiderpublishing.com

GLASS
SPIDER
PUBLISHING

Local Queer Resources

Co-owner of Laziz Kitchen, Moudi Sbeity, has partnered with the founder of River Writing, Nan Seymour, to create a safe space for local queers & allies in Salt Lake City, Utah. On the last Sunday of each month, he hosts Queer Poetry Night at his restaurant from 7-9pm. To find out more about this event, you can check out the social media accounts for Laziz Kitchen SLC as well as go directly to the River Writing events page.

www.lazizkitchen.com
www.riverwriting.com

UTAH
pride
CENTER

Utah Pride Center is a nonprofit organization that supports & serves the Utah LGBTQIA2S+ community and its allies.

www.utahpridecenter.org

Encircle is a nonprofit organization that provides support & counseling for LGBTQ+ students and their families at multiple locations in Utah.

www.encircletogether.org

Project Rainbow

Project Rainbow works to promote LGBTQ+ visibility throughout Utah and foster inclusivity in every corner of the state.

www.projectrainbowutah.org

Under the
Umbrella
A QUEER LITTLE BOOKSTORE

As of November 2021, Salt Lake City has a new bookstore & it's totally queer.

www.undertheumbrellabookstore.com

Full Circle Yoga & Therapy is a safe, inclusive
space to work out both your body & mind.

www.fullcircleut.com

Local Cat & Pizza Resources

tinkerscatcafe
SLC's first CAT CAFE ☕ Cafe Tues-Sun 9am 🐱
CAT LOUNGE IS OPEN Tues-Thurs 10-6pm Fri-
Sat 10-7 Sun 11-6 CLOSED MONDAYS

This is where to go to pet all the freakin'
adorable cats that are up for adoption & to
drink delicious cat-themed coffee or tea to boot.

www.tinkerscatcafe.com

I know this isn't original but: adopt, don't shop.

www.utahhumane.org
www.bestfriends.org/sanctuary
utah.bestfriends.org

There are too many amazing pizza places in the Salt Lake City metro area to list. Taste all the delicious pizza available everywhere.